T0159055

Ebullience

Vishaldeep Sanghera

authorHOUSE®

AuthorHouse™
1663 Liberty Drive
Bloomington, IN 47403
www.authorhouse.com
Phone: 1 (800) 839-8640

Published by AuthorHouse 11/29/2018

ISBN: 978-1-5462-6724-9 (sc)
ISBN: 978-1-5462-6723-2 (e)

Library of Congress Control Number: 2018913411

Print information available on the last page.

Stepping In

Why must it seem
That inspiration is a random act of nature
Striking as if lightning; but formed as ideas
Shot off from far reaches of other dimensions
To collect into a nascent discovery
By the one who bears to interpret it

The residual After-effects

What's left?
When one love has left physically
The other stayed, but diverged in thoughts and memories?
Which would seem to be the worse form of trickery?
The heart wants faint whispers of love translated eagerly
As bad as it needs
The rhythm of two bodies humming in corners peacefully

Today's Distraction

Today's Distraction
Serves to cause the mind satisfaction
A natural borne reaction
To utter boredom and squander the here-and-now moments

Today's Distraction
Is where this generation wants to wander
Affixed to screens, the minds ponder
To numb senses and let "the drugs" loot & plunder

Today's Distraction
It instinctively feels so right
Deeply ingrained to be up all night
To play all-in, if for just the short sight

Today's Distraction
Because only the cosmos out there know
What could be done by Man if he were to grow
And down the path less traveled, he would go

Today's Distraction

Today's distraction is one disguised as gold
The pace of the long journey is the one we should hold
Today is the battleground for the day of tomorrow
And that's a story, I've heard many times told

Are We Human?

A Father is supposed to be the "rock", the purveyor
A Mother scolds as much as she holds you in prayers
But are we both not human?

American kids concerned with getting an education
An African child contemplating tonight's starvation
But are we both not human?

Car enthusiasts fantasize over the latest model
The self-proclaimed connoisseur wrapped around an IPA
bottle
But are we both not human?

The adventurer has tales of the trails that are taken
One who's lost love knows of a life forsaken
But are we both not human?

The soldier knows of camaraderie with brothers
The new Mom's full grasp of love when she sees her child
and no other
But are we both not human?

Shorts x1

If our Aim is to connect at first,
With anyone we meet
Wouldn't life be a bit more vibrant?
And wouldn't we hold a better view from our seat?

Fertile Soil

To the person this is dedicated to
You know who you are
Just know if you need me
I'll never be too far
Why do we get caught up in the craziness of this world?
The economical, the financial, in other words stressful.
And take our eyes off of our premiere duty?
It's really not that hard
Trying to comprehend this "life" thing

Just know that whatever has been planted.
Will need to a little water to grow
For the seed will surely sprout, high & full of life
And I aim to care for it until I'm old & slow
Just as the saying goes
You shall reap
Only that, which you sow

And just know that deep in your heart
And in your blood; You Are Royal
And that you are my seed
And for you, I am the Soil.

Astronomer vs. Astronaut

Astronomer vs. Astronaut
3D vs. Life
Chemical vs. Organic
Silver-spoon vs. Strife

Produce vs. Packaging
Footprints vs. Movie Reel
Trails vs. Pages
Human Senses vs. Green-Screen Appeal

Raw & Pure vs Derivative
Nutrition vs. Supplementation
Sentient vs Artificial
Creation vs Exaggeration

Hard Shell of Love

So obsessed with everything draping the exterior
When fear I hold inside, and feel inferior
The only way to vocalize what I feel
To say it spans the far reaches of Superior

Still I know, it's the surface that's entranced me
Innocence that envelopes all of which is disastrous
Casting spells that will for sure subdue me
But I guess I'm still looking for some purity

Poetry

Don't mind if it sounds like rap
Can't discern if it's fully poetry
The pictures painted by these words
Is the only thing, sometimes that's showing me
Lending to navigate through inevitable fissures
Helping to speak, when I can't find my voice
Hope these words do something for you
Maybe give some power; maybe choice
To realize that even if you're feeling low
And all your dreams are fairy tales spun high
Just to realize that you will overcome this struggle
And I know that like I know the shape of the sky
I know that as truth from the bottom of my heart
And you don't have to be perfect to change
Just start
Because I know what a few words… Just a few
Can help alter a reality from facades to truth
Can do the extraordinary for the likes of us
Just simply listen; you have unimaginable talent within you

Shorts x2

I think we all have it, this disorder
To shy away and play average
And why would you hide stuff away- you're not a hoarder?

Speak your most brilliant thoughts
Express your deepest meanings and feelings
And live this life without any borders

Shorts x3

Even if your body aches
I hope your mind doesn't
My hope is you never get caught in material
But rather drift away in imagination and substance

Promises

Nothing is as cheap as words
Nothing so easy to provide the heart bliss
That's maybe why those promises that you've heard
Are as real the fountain you stop at to make a wish
Yet, I find a way to show you some hope
Piece together some stitching of trust
"I've changed, I know I can be the man you need"
Still blurring the lines between love and lust

But there's a chance, a faint glimmer hope
From time to time, I carry through action
But we're miles away, on the inside
And maybe I'm in chase of momentary satisfaction
So the promises that have been made until now
The "I'm dead serious, it'll be different"-isms
Are escaping and fading away to nothingness

I think you should escape
For once I speak wisdom

Lucrative (Rat Race)

Who am I doing this for?
Unguided, uninstructed, not sure where the road goes
And who determined the destination??
Better yet, whose destination are we trying to get to?
The paper-printers, the lenders, the creditors
The financial institutions or bustling markets?
The media, the news channels, the radio ads
The ones who cut the checks or help your debts
Is the picture enlarging?
Take a step back to analyze the whole puzzle
Running from one end to another
To get some green on this side to be relay-race it
To the runner on the other side, a few strides ahead
And lap after lap, mile after mile
You keep clocking in with faster times
But whose race are you running all this while??

Shorts x4

It's
all just stepping-stones..
Until
you fully realize your Dream
Then
acquire the toolbelt necessary
To
come to actualize your Dream...

Morning Energy

The most dreaded time
By most of the populous
It's society's programming

Don't you see?
Morning is another opportunity at life
One more chance to make your reality
To do it better than it's ever been done before

And doesn't the sunrise recharge you after the night?
It's a rebirth; an awakening of the Earth
And a new birth for you

To plant new seeds
To grow a new and never before seen life...
Treat the mornings as much

Less Words... More Meaning...

I want my poetry
To talk, to chatter
To scream from the tops of mountains
And shake the Earth in violent upheavals

Shorts X5

How many hours, minutes, seconds..
How many days?
How many countless times I wandered

But I found you
Now would it be wrong?
To say my path ends where you stood still
If even for a second?

Simplicity

Simplicity
Such a difficult word
Entrenching the secret within it's sound
The simple lies inside the difficult
This is what I have found

Passion (Pandora's Box)

Most people will take the wrong angle
When reading this title
This is not be sensationalized
Or tuned to the sphere of physicality
This truly is about definitive passion

Trapped
Untapped
Unsurfaced

To weather away like leaves in autumn
Or better even, like hidden treasure in the sands

Because who knows might would happen
If you were to dig into that passion and hold on feverishly
But for eons till now, it remains a secret
Pandora's Box

Contextual

Aimless wanderlust
Many trips
Drifting oh so sweetly in the breeze
Whichever way the jet streams see it be
There's a lightness to it all, but an emptiness
It's like being constantly steered off course
Sometimes, unquestionably to paradise
But other times to pain and remorse
It's like the compass stays broken
So how am I supposed to know where I'm going?
Departures are many
But alas, it'd be extraordinary to know where I might settle
The meaning to this journey seems like it's missing
Context needed to understand the travel plans

Ebullience

The archetype of a child
The only known behavior of toddlers & infants

That fear
That despair
That uncertainty

You see that's what this world taught you
It's the fabrication of actual existence
A facsimile of another's life pointed at you, not your own

The truth, you see, lies in your inside
On the other side of the paper-thin wall of fear
So go Uncover that truth
The truth the younger you already knew
The kid in you still knows

You were birthed an original
You were not born to be stopped

Tree of Wisdom

The thick, mangled roots
With old rusty fibers and hairs
Spreading & stretching to the deepest reaches of the Earth
Tracing elaborate patterns through the soil
The bark, telling a tale of its own hieroglyphic artistry
Plastered width, year after year

Hiding the stories of the forest and it's past seasons
Wonder what these ancient giants have seen?

The bulk of the trunk, circling a circumference so wide
A fortitude so mighty that no animal
Could withstand to it
Weathered and overcame seasons of nature's intentions
Often changing direction and growing in detours
In the case of obstruction or interruptions

What magnitude of patience does it take?
What inevitable wisdom acquired along the path??

Survivor

Whatever you're going through
Rest easy, knowing that you'll make it through
It's not an experience to break you; but a lesson to make you
You'll be the father you're meant to me
You'll be the mother you're meant to be
It might not be easy to see with the current lens muddy
One day you'll look back and laugh at the absurdity

Because by the you will have already become the figure
You already will have become the guide
So you can assure the younger "you" from days past
That that kid no longer has to hide

Thirst

How badly I want to make it onto these pages
If you could only sense the fire that lies deep
A fiery, insatiable inferno
Don't confuse it, however
It's not anger
Not even desire or drive
It's a thirst
A thirst I need to quench in order to feel alive!
It's not enough for me to survive
I want to pay the sacrifice needed to succeed
The resistance offers me no trouble
I'll pull my dream into a reality even you can see

Deep down
I know, I'm a far-fetched dreamer
And because I sense it in my heart
And I know it's mine from the start

Shorts x6

I've been trying to recognize myself
In the mirror I point towards everybody
Trying to make sense of these reflections
Just to find out that you are me

Shorts x7

Is there really love, without sacrifice?
And has there ever been sacrifice, if not for love?

About the Author

Vishaldeep Sanghera works as an Accounts Receivable Coordinator in southern Washington state. He graduated from Washington State University in 2015 at Pullman, Washington and comes from a business background. Vishaldeep was born in India, immigrated to the United States at the age of 2.5 years and lived in the Pacific Northwest ever since. There's a certain dichotomy to this publication because although the author works in accounting, this work aims to unsurfaced and touch the unseen, the emotional, and everything beneath the surface of the skin.

Printed in the United States
By Bookmasters